T0170605

THE BOOK OF REPULSIVE

DJUNA CHAPPELL BARNES was born in Cornwall-on-Hudson in 1892. She grew up in an eccentric, polygamous household, and was educated at home by her suffragist grandmother. She moved to New York in 1911, where she briefly studied at the Pratt Institute of Art, and where she made her living as a writer, penning feature articles, short stories, one-act dramas and poetry. Barnes was a talented artist who illustrated her own work throughout her life. In the 1920s she moved to Paris, where she lived and worked amongst the literary expatriate community until the late 1930s, when she moved back to New York. Barnes is most famous for her 1936 novel *Nightwood* but her three other major works, *Ryder* (1928), *Ladies Almanack* (1928) and *The Antiphon* (1958), are arguably as important. In her later years Barnes became reclusive, refusing public attention and attempts to republish her work. She died in 1982 at the age of ninety.

REBECCA LONCRAINE wrote her doctoral thesis on Djuna Barnes' New York writing. From 2002 to 2003 she was a research fellow at the Rothermere American Institute at the University of Oxford, where she worked on early twentieth-century American literature and film.

Fyfield*Books* aim to make available some of the great classics of British and European literature in clear, affordable formats, and to restore often neglected writers to their place in literary tradition.

Fyfield*Books* take their name from the Fyfield elm in Matthew Arnold's 'Scholar Gypsy' and 'Thyrsis'. The tree stood not far from the village where the series was originally devised in 1971.

> *Roam on! The light we sought is shining still.*
> *Dost thou ask proof? Our tree yet crowns the hill,*
> *Our Scholar travels yet the loved hill-side*

from 'Thyrsis'

DJUNA BARNES

The Book of
Repulsive Women
and other poems

Edited with an introduction by
REBECCA LONCRAINE

Fyfield*Books*

CARCANET

First published in Great Britain in 2003 by
Carcanet Press Limited
Alliance House
Cross Street
Manchester M2 7AQ

A CIP catalogue record for this book is available from the British Library
ISBN 1 85754 707 1

The publisher acknowledges financial assistance from Arts Council England

Typeset by XL Publishing Services, Tiverton

CONTENTS

INTRODUCTION

Revelling grandly into vice
Dropping crooked into rhyme.
Slipping through the stitch of virtue

Djuna Barnes once described herself as the most famous unknown writer. To an extent she was right. Her name is familiar to many, especially to those with an interest in early twentieth-century literature, but her work is not (yet) widely read. She is best known for her 1936 novella *Nightwood*, published by Faber & Faber under the editorial guidance of T.S. Eliot. This work is rightly regarded as her masterpiece, but she did write much else besides.

Ironically, Barnes was herself partially responsible for her lack of readership. Before her death in 1982 at the age of ninety, many editors and publishers had approached her to request the republication of her earlier work, but she flatly refused, putting a stop to all attempts at bringing out new collections or editions of her writing. She tried to get the New York bookstore 'Djuna Books' to change its name, she refused to let a mime troupe do an interpretation of *Nightwood*, and she even shunned numerous requests for the film rights to the story, including an overture from Ingmar Bergman. Barnes' reply to a questionnaire sent by *The Little Review* to 'the artists of the world', was simply, 'I am sorry but the list of questions does not interest me to answer. Nor have I that respect for the public.' In the latter years of her life she seemed determined to keep herself out of print (and out of pocket). She has become known as the Greta Garbo of American letters – reclusive, bohemian, sexually ambiguous and extraordinarily glamorous. Strangely, rumour has it that she would have given Bergman the rights to make *Nightwood* if he had cast Garbo as the lead.

Since her death, there has been a considerable effort by publishers to ignore Barnes' wishes and republish her work. Collections of her prose, drama, short stories and drawings have appeared, but as yet no edition of her poetry has been published. This collection brings together most of Djuna Barnes' poetry, both published and unpublished, for the first time.

Barnes was born in Cornwall-on-Hudson, New York, in 1892, and brought up on a farm in an unconventional, some would say dysfunctional, family. Her father Wald was a failed artist and a polygamist. She lived with her mother, father, brothers, grandmother, and Wald's other 'wife' Fanny, and her children, also by him. The Barnes children were all educated at home, largely by their grandmother, Zadel Barnes, who was a suffragist, journalist and spirit medium. Her childhood was not happy, and it would haunt both her life and writing. She would write complex and furious accounts of family life in her 1928 novel *Ryder* and her 1958 play *The Antiphon*.

In 1912 Barnes moved to New York City with her mother and brothers, where she joined the Pratt Institute of Art. She studied there for several months before money shortages forced her to look for work. She began working as a cub writer and illustrator for the *Brooklyn Daily Eagle*, reporting on local crime and courtroom hearings. In 1913, Carl Van Vechten hired her to write for the *New York Press*, where she wrote theatre reviews and interviews, meeting some of the celebrities of the day, including Lillian Russell and Florenz Zeigfeld. She began working for the *New York World* in 1914, writing stunt features about her experiences as a dummy body for trainee fire fighters, and, most shockingly, about the experience of being force fed. In the light of the imprisonment and force-feeding of the British suffragettes, Barnes had agreed to undergo this ordeal, and she wrote about it in touching and gruesome detail in a piece entitled simply, 'How it Feels to be Forcibly Fed'. She also developed a fascination with boxing. Women had only recently been admitted to boxing matches and she embraced this new opportunity for spectacle with relish. She interviewed Jack Dempsey and Jess Willard and wrote several articles about her experiences attending bouts.

In 1915 Barnes moved to Greenwich Village, where she lived until 1921, mingling with the bohemian and artistic community for which it was famous. She did, however, retain a certain distance from this crowd, writing satirical articles about 'bohemia', such as 'Becoming Intimate with the Bohemians' and 'How the Villagers Amuse Themselves' for New York's daily press. She joined the Little Theatre movement, writing and performing in plays with the Provincetown Players. She had numerous love affairs with both men and women, and was briefly married to Courtenay Lemon, a political radical and journalist. One of her lovers, a German named Putzi Hanfstaengl, saved Barnes' life. The editor of the *New York World* had planned to send her up in a homemade aeroplane, as one of the first women to fly. Hanfstaengl convinced her not to go and gave her the twenty-five dollars she would have earned from the article recounting the stunt. The aeroplane crashed, killing all on board.

In 1921 *McCalls Magazine* sent Barnes to Paris to write a series of articles on American expatriate life in the city. She spent the next ten years in Europe, primarily in Paris, where she mixed with the artistic expatriate community, including Mabel Dodge, Marcel Duchamp, Man Ray and Gertrude Stein. One of her closest friends at this time was the poet Mina Loy, who lived with her two daughters in the same building as Barnes. Barnes continued to work for American magazines and journals, interviewing writers and artists, including F. Scott Fitzgerald and James Joyce. She even interviewed Coco Chanel, the woman 'world famous for two things, perfume and severe-tailored suits'. It is a testament to Barnes' growing fame as a writer during these years that Fitzgerald remarked during his interview, 'My God, I should be interviewing you.'

While she was in Paris, Barnes befriended the beneficent patrons Natalie Barney and Peggy Guggenheim, who would support her with literary stipends in years to come. She also met Thelma Wood, a silverpoint artist, with whom she had a notoriously tumultuous relationship, which lasted for the next ten years. Wood's infidelities tortured Barnes and she began drinking heavily. By 1929 the painful relationship with Wood was over, and Barnes moved briefly back to New York. She then spent some time travelling around Europe and North Africa, before moving permanently back to New York and into Patchin Place in Greenwich Village, where she lived a relatively reclusive life until her death. Her neighbour was the poet e.e. cummings, but by all accounts they rarely spoke to one another.

Barnes was a creative jack-of-all-trades. She wrote successfully in a number of genres and was an accomplished painter and illustrator as well. She produced short stories, journalism, drama, two novels and illustrated much of her own work. However, she had made her literary debut as a poet. In 1915 she published her first book, a series of eight poems, or 'rhythms' as she called them, accompanied by five drawings (which are reproduced here). It is this small pamphlet, entitled *The Book of Repulsive Women*, from which this present collection takes its title. It became an underground classic, not least for its sexual explicitness about love between women, which somehow got past the censors. Published a full decade before Radclyffe Hall's *The Well of Loneliness*, it was the first modern work to bring 'the love that dare not speak its name' explicitly into verse. Barnes' biographer Andrew Field has suggested that, like Queen Victoria before them, the censors obviously 'could not even imagine the offence'.

In 1923 Barnes published a collection of poems, short stories and one-act plays entitled simply *A Book*. In 1928 she published two of her best works. *Ryder* is a bawdy biography of her family, written in mock Elizabethan verse combined with Joycean wordplay. Like an early graphic novel, it is illustrated throughout with captioned, witty illustrations. To Barnes' horror the book was severely censored, its many references to bodily functions excised. She refused to rewrite any of it and instead merely inserted asterisks where the censors had made cuts, so that the reader could, in her own words, 'see the havoc of this nicety'. In the same year she published the extraordinary *Ladies Almanack*, which was also composed in mock Elizabethan English. Written anonymously by 'A Lady of Fashion' as an unconventional almanac for 'Ladies', it is a beautifully illustrated, hilarious and ribald account of the lesbian literary expatriate community in Paris, with which Barnes mingled at this time. The book was sold to friends, mainly those who were mocked in its pages. Barnes famously shunned sexual categorisation, asserting, 'I am not a lesbian, I just loved Thelma', and her work raises important questions concerning identity. Despite her characteristic claim that she wrote *Ladies Almanack* 'in an idle hour', as a 'jollity' for a 'very special audience', the book engages with questions of sexuality in intriguing ways. Since its posthumous republication it has become a cult classic.

Barnes' best known work, *Nightwood*, appeared in 1936. Many have read it as a meditation on her broken relationship with Thelma Wood, a tale of love and loss in between-the-wars Europe, in an atmosphere of drink, drugs, shell shock and spiralling anti-Semitism. After the publication of *Nightwood* Barnes settled in New York, where her creative output dwindled until the 1950s, when she published a play, *The Antiphon*. In this dark and difficult drama, she revisited her childhood once again, to produce a dense and unrelenting attack on family life. Her poem 'Solitude' seems to encapsulate the impetus behind *The Antiphon*:

> This is my perfect solitude
> Within my conquering abode,
> The goal of haunting memories
> That walk beside a chartless road.

The play premiered at Stockholm's Royal Dramatic Theatre in 1961. From the 1960s until her death Barnes concentrated on writing poetry, little of which has been published until now.

Though known primarily as a writer of prose and drama, Barnes' has arguably had most influence on poets. In his introduction to her work, T.S. Eliot wrote, '*Nightwood* will appeal primarily to readers of poetry… it is so good a novel that only sensibilities trained on poetry can wholly appreciate it.' The book has often been read as a prose-poem, which suggests that Barnes should be understood primarily as a poet.

This collection contains poems written across the wide span of her long career. They appear in chronological order, beginning with work composed in New York and published in literary journals and magazines such as *Harper's Weekly*, the *All-Story Cavalier Weekly*, *The Dial* and *Smart Set*. The poems that follow appeared in the 1915 pamphlet *The Book of Repulsive Women*, and in the 1923 collection *A Book*. While in Paris, Barnes continued to write poems for American magazines and literary journals such as *Vanity Fair*, *Shadowland* and *New Republic*. The collection ends with the posthumously published *Creatures in an Alphabet*, followed by some of the unpublished Patchin Place poems, which were mainly written after 1960.

In a letter to her friend Emily Coleman, Barnes observed, 'there is always more surface to a shattered object than a whole'. Her poems, written over a period of sixty or so years, inevitably exhibiting considerable change and development in form, style and influence. The early poems are reminiscent of Emily Dickinson and Christina Rossetti, while the later work looks further back to John Donne and the metaphysical poets. In certain respects this diverse collection is a shattered object; it is made up of pieces from very different periods of Barnes' life and work. Despite this, the poems are in many ways thematically consistent. 'Seen from the "L"', one of the 'rhythms' from the 1915 pamphlet *The Book of Repulsive Women*, is characteristic. Barnes uses a startling range of metaphors, juxtaposing images and concepts that jar and jolt the reader. A line from the poem, 'Dropping crooked into rhyme', is an apt description of Barnes' writing as a whole. Her poems often produce a shocking verbal and cognitive dissonance, particularly at line endings, where she introduces entirely unexpected images. The idea of 'cuttle and costard on a plate' in 'Discant (There should be gardens)'; her description of a flock of birds as 'a shower of glass' in 'Portrait of a Lady Walking'; or the image of 'Corpse B' in 'Suicide' lying 'listlessly like some small mug / Of beer gone flat', are good examples. These deliberately incongruous images refashion one's perception of objects and events, enabling one to 'sense things are not as they are', as Barnes put it in 'The Yellow Jar'.

'Seen from the "L"', which seems to allude to Keats' 'Ode on a Grecian Urn' (1820), can be read as a comment on Barnes' own writing:

> Though her lips are vague and fancy
> In her youth –
> They bloom vivid and repulsive
> As the truth.
> Even vases in the making
> Are uncouth.

Her use of 'repulsive' is significant. The images of the body in her work, often rotting, decaying or ill-fitting, are grotesque. 'This flesh laid on us like a wrinkled glove', she writes in 'The Lament of Women'. Throughout her poetry, she is preoccupied with images of the body, and especially of corpses. Her poems present live bodies as decaying flesh, while corpses have a perverse vitality. Her muse is a dead woman. 'The Flowering Corpse' is a good example:

> Over the body and the quiet head
> Like stately ferns above an austere tomb,
> Soft hairs blow; and beneath her armpits bloom
> The drowsy passion flowers of the dead.

In 'Suicide', 'Corpse A' is 'a little bruised body like / A startled moon'; in 'Love Song' the 'I' of the poem is 'A corpse that flames and cannot die'. Dead women are the addressees of 'Lines to a Lady' and 'To the Dead Favourite of Liu Ch'e'. Barnes wants to repulse but also attract the reader with deliberately unnerving imagery. What makes it all the more effective is that, as in Christina

Rossetti, there is a *faux naïveté* to her work. 'Lullaby', for example, shocks with its nursery rhyme voice discussing suicide: 'Now I lie here with my eyes on a pistol'.

Dolly Wilde once warned Barnes that people who spend too much time alone are in danger of turning into enormous ears, and this seems to have happened to Barnes, who in 'The Lament of Women' writes of a love of 'This pale, this over eager listening ear'. She uses musical terms throughout her writing: 'discant', for example, used in the title of several poems, is another term for 'descant', meaning 'a decorative counterpoint added above a basic melody'. Her repeated references to feet, to beats, and to sounds, are perhaps attempts to draw our attention to the metrical rhythms and movements of her verse. In 'Seen from the "L"' the mosaic of light outside the window 'Is scribbled there by tipsy sparrows – / Etched there with their rocking feet. / Is fashioned too, by every beat / Of shirt and sheet'. In 'Lullaby' Barnes 'planted pepper-seed and stamped on / them hard'; 'White butterflies lift up their furry feet' in 'Pastoral', and 'In Conclusion' reads, 'Some hour the echo of our feet will flee'. In 'The Dreamer', Barnes' first published poem, she writes of rain that 'softly patters by, like little fearing feet.' Often the metrical rhythms of her verse are at odds with the dissonance of her imagery, adding to the fascinating 'crookedness' of her writing.

Marianne Moore enjoyed Barnes' work, and remarked, 'reading Djuna Barnes is like reading a foreign language, which you understand'. Reading her is certainly a disorientating experience, as Moore points out. Her kind of writing demands effort and several readings, but with time it provokes a 'seeing anew', the mark of all good poetry, that is both repellent and compelling. These poems demonstrate that Barnes should be taken seriously as a poet, as well as a writer of prose and drama. They add a further dimension to her oeuvre, and throw new light on her development as a writer. Her work is haunted by the past, by memory and by irrevocable loss. In 'Rite of Spring' she comments on this when she writes:

> Man cannot purge his body of its theme
> As can the silkworm on a running thread
> Spin a shroud to re-consider in.

Barnes' poetry can be seen as a cocoon, spun in an attempt to create a space for reflection and consideration. It is my hope that this collection will contribute to the process of unknotting something of her past, by challenging her view of herself as the most famous unknown writer; to make her, if not more famous, then at least a little less unknown.

Acknowledgements

This project would not have been possible without the generosity of the Rothermere American Institute at the University of Oxford. I would also like to thank Ben Brice, Trisha Loncraine, Joe Luscombe, Mina Gorji, Yasmin Khan, and Farrhat Arshad for their help and support.

SOURCES

Texts of the poems are based on the following sources:

'The Dreamer', *Harper's Weekly*, LV, 24 June 1911

'Call of the Night', *Harper's Weekly*, LV, 23 December 1911

'Just Lately Drummer Boy', *The Trend*, VIII, October 1914

'"Six Carried Her Away"', *The Trend*, VIII, November 1914

'Solitude', *All-Story Cavalier Weekly*, XXXIX, 28 November 1914

'The Personal God', *The Trend*, VIII, December 1914

'Jungle Jargon', in Barnes' article, 'Djuna Barnes Probes the Souls of Jungle Folk at the Hippodrome Circus', *New York Press*, 14 February 1915

'This Much and More', *All-Story Cavalier Weekly*, XLIX, 4 September 1915

From Fifth Avenue Up', *The Book of Repulsive Women: 8 Rhythms and 5 Drawings*. Bruno's Chapbooks, II, No. 6, November 1915

'In General', *The Book of Repulsive Women*, 1915

'From Third Avenue On', *The Book of Repulsive Women*, 1915

'Seen From the "L"', *The Book of Repulsive Women*, 1915

'In Particular', *The Book of Repulsive Women*, 1915

'Twilight of the Illicit', *The Book of Repulsive Women*, 1915

'To a Cabaret Dancer', *The Book of Repulsive Women*, 1915

'Suicide', *The Book of Repulsive Women*, 1915

'Death', *All-Story Cavalier Weekly*, LV, 4 March 1916

'In Conclusion', *All-Story Cavalier Weekly*, LVII, 6 May 1916

'Dust', *All-Story Cavalier Weekly*, 3 June 1916

'Birth', *All-Story Cavalier Weekly*, 24 June 1916

'The Yellow Jar', *Munsey's Magazine*, LVIII, September 1916

'The Last Toast', *All-Story Cavalier Weekly*, LXII, 9 September 1916

'To an Idol', *All-Story Cavalier Weekly*, LXII, 16 September 1916

'Shadows', *Munsey's Magazine*, LIX, November 1916

'Love Song', *All-Story Cavalier Weekly*, LXIX, 18 November 1916

'Lines to a Lady', *All-Story Cavalier Weekly*, LXXXIV, 1 June 1918

'The Lament of Women', *Little Review*, V, December 1918

'To the Hands of a Beloved', *All-Story Cavalier Weekly*, XCVII, 17 May 1919

'To One in Favour', *Smart Set*, LIX, July 1919

'To a Bird', *All-Story Cavalier Weekly*, CI, 20 September 1919

'To the Dead Favourite of Liu Ch'e', *The Dial*, LXVII, April 1920

'To One Feeling Differently', *Playboy*, II, March 1923

'She Passed This Way', *Vanity Fair*, XX, March 1923

'Crystals', *New Republic*, XXXV, 20 June 1923

'The Child Would Be Older', *Shadowland*, VIII, July 1923

'To One in Another Mood', *Vanity Fair*, XXI, November 1923

'I'd Have You Think of Me', *A Book*, New York: Boni & Liveright, 1923

'The Flowering Corpse', *A Book*, 1923

'Song in Autumn', *A Book*, 1923.

'First Communion', *A Book*, 1923

'Hush Before Love', *A Book*, 1923

'Antique', *A Book*, 1923

'Pastoral', *A Book*, 1923

'Paradise', *A Book*, 1923

'Six Songs of Khalidine', *A Book*, 1923

'Lullaby', *A Book*, 1923

'Finis', *A Book*, 1923

'Quarry', *New Yorker*, 45, 27 December 1969

'The Walking-Mort', *New Yorker*, 47, 15 May 1971

'Rite of Spring', *Grand Street*, Spring 1982

'Creatures in an Alphabet', New York: Dial Press, 1982

'When the Kissing Flesh is Gone'. Date unknown. Unpublished manuscript, University of Maryland

'Portrait of a Lady Walking'. Date unknown. Unpublished manuscript, University of Maryland

'Lament For Wretches, Every One'. Date unknown. Unpublished manuscript, University of Maryland.

'As Cried'. Date unknown. Unpublished manuscript, University of Maryland

'As Cried'. Date unknown. Unpublished manuscript, University of Maryland

'Discant (There should be gardens)'. Date unknown. Unpublished manuscript, University of Maryland

'Satires (Satires of Don Pasquin)'. Date unknown. Unpublished manuscript, University of Maryland

'Discontent'. Date unknown. Unpublished manuscript, University of Maryland

'Dereliction'. Date unknown. Unpublished manuscript, University of Maryland

FURTHER READING

Works by Djuna Barnes

The Antiphon: A Play. London: Faber & Faber, 1958

At the Roots of the Stars: The Short Plays. Los Angeles: Sun & Moon Press, 1995

A Book. New York: Boni & Liveright, 1923

The Book of Repulsive Women: 8 Rhythms and 5 Drawings. Bruno's Chapbooks, II, No. 6, November 1915. Reprinted Los Angeles: Sun and Moon Press, 1994

The Collected Stories of Djuna Barnes. Los Angeles: Sun and Moon Press, 1996

Creatures in an Alphabet. New York: Dial Press, 1982

Greenwich Village as It Is. New York: Phoenix Bookshop, 1978

I Could Never Be Lonely without a Husband: Interviews. London: Virago, 1987

Interviews. Los Angeles: Sun & Moon Press, 1985

Ladies Almanack. Dijon, France: privately printed, 1928. Reprinted New York: New York University Press, 1992

New York. Los Angeles: Sun and Moon Press, 1989

A Night Among the Horses. New York: Boni & Liveright, 1929

Nightwood. London: Faber & Faber, 1936. Reprinted London: Faber & Faber, 1995

Ryder. New York: Boni & Liveright, 1928. Reprinted Normal, IL.: Dalkey Archive Press, 1990

Selected Works of Djuna Barnes. London: Faber & Faber, 1962

Smoke, and Other Early Stories. London: Virago, 1985

Spillway. London: Faber & Faber, 1962

Other Reading

Benstock, Shari. *Women of the Left Bank*. London: Virago, 1986
   An informative and entertaining account of Barnes and her literary milieu in the Paris of the 1920s

Broe, Mary Lynn, ed., *Silence and Power: A Reevaluation of Djuna Barnes*. Carbondale: Southern Illinois University Press, 1991
   A useful collection of excellent essays on Barnes which covers

a range of her writings and takes an interesting variety of approaches to Barnes' work

Field, Andrew. *The Formidable Miss Barnes*. London: Secker & Warburg, 1983

The first Barnes biography. It is fun and engaging, if a little out of date now

Herring, Phillip. *Djuna: The Life and Works of Djuna Barnes*. New York: Penguin Books, 1995

The most recent biography of Barnes, thorough and perceptive

Messerli, Douglas. *Djuna Barnes: A Bibliography*. Rhinebeck: D. Lewis, 1975

A useful bibliography of both Barnes' work and secondary material on Barnes, though it only goes up to 1975, and the most interesting work on Barnes has been written after this date

The Dreamer

The night comes down, in ever-darkening shapes that
      seem –
To grope, with eerie fingers for the window – then –
To rest, to sleep, enfolding me, as in a dream.
          Faith – might I waken!

And drips the rain with seeming sad, insistent
      beat.
Shivering across the pane, drooping tear-wise,
And softly patters by, like little fearing feet.
          Faith –'tis weather!

The feathery ash is fluttered: there upon the
      pane, –
The dying fire casts a flickering ghostly beam, –
Then closes in the night and gently falling rain.
          Faith – what darkness!

Call of the Night

Dark, and the wind-blurred pines.
   With a glimmer of light between.
Then I, entombed for an hourless night
   With the world of things unseen.

Mist, the dust of flowers,
   Leagues, heavy with promise of snow,
And a beckoning road 'twixt vale and hill.
   With the lure that all must know.

A light, my window's gleam,
   Soft, flaring its squares of red –
I lose the ache of the wilderness
   And long for the fire instead.

You too know, old fellow?
   Then, lift up your head and bark.
It's just the call of the lonesome place,
   The winds and the housing dark.

Just Lately Drummer Boy

His face is set with parapet
    Of tears that come too soon.
He has no drum, and so he plays
    Upon a pallid moon.
There is no music in his heart
    Yet he makes a little tune.

The soldiers walk, the soldiers stalk
    Like terrible gray wheat.
And as they walk they make no sound,
    They move on phantom feet.
Incomplete their vestments are
    Their mission incomplete.

And so they pass, dim in the grass
    Outcome of shot and shell.
He has no music in his heart
    And yet he plays quite well.
Perhaps his music-master is
    Just lately – Israel.

'Six Carried Her Away'

They rode the car with spade,
With pickaxe and with blade,
To shape a grave, new made
    Wherein a girl must lie.

She gave the good of gain,
And suffered life's great pain,
And in the hour of rain, –
    Her call it came, to die.

She'd filled the barren street
With sound of wanton feet,
Advancing, till retreat
    Was asked of her, as pay.

And all who'd sought her out
In horror turned about,
For death is sick with doubt,
    Six carried her away.

Six men complete her fall;
Just six more feet, that's all;
Six feet of earth's good pall;
    For this they dig the wet.

She knew no future lease
On death's fine brand of peace
Could bring her mind's release,
    Nor would her soul forget.

'Neath sky gone blank of stars
They fly the dancing cars,
And shoulder pick and bars,
    And hum a low refrain.

Bravely, here stretch her feet
Above that still, complete
Drab water winding sheet
    With border wet with rain.

Into the gaping park
Trailed round with lantern spark
They come, half hid by dark
    And half revealed by dawn.

They, from the rain-steeped town
From swinging boards drop down,
In grey of mist, and brown
    Of umber earth undone.

Of stalwart build and drape,
Till the mist reclaims their shape
With twist of foggy crepe,
    And all of them are – none.

Solitude

I seek no solitude but this –
   This one within my little room –
Four candles set apart to watch
   With wistful eyes the coming gloom.

And this, the shrouded mantelpiece
   And sober gap of fireside-place;
And this, the darkened wonder of
   A framed picture of a face.

This is my perfect solitude
   Within my conquering abode,
The goal of haunting memories
   That walk beside a chartless road

The Personal God

Creeds of a kind we've always had
To crouch by our dim fireside.
And here some gossiping wench arose
And the worth of some good name died;
Yea, the whole stale world went rocking
To the sting of her poisoned heels,
As a sky-car mangles the stars
For lack of the guiding wheels.
Though all of us sin most fully
When hushed in our neighborly sweats,
Yet sometimes a man goes empty
For the urge of things, and forgets.
We stick to the same old pattern,
All daubed and kissed and marred,
But I'll use my own gray plaster
And I'll build me a personal God.
I'll breathe out his flaccid belly,
I'll cup out his sightless eyes,
I'll sob in the labor bending,
As I handle his plastic thighs.
And he shall be rash of judgment,
And slow in the use of the rod.
My God shall giggle in spite of himself,
In the way of a personal God.
He shall heed no other's message;
He shall follow no dusty path;
He'll believe in no written pity;
Nor yet in a written wrath;
He'll breed no circle of platters
Nor take root in your yearly fees;
He'll ask no patient toll of tears
Nor the terrible toll of the knees.
So, when all of you flock to your fancy,
The God that is always the same,
My God shall halt and be human
And his judgment shall halt and be lame.
Yea, the devil came down your pass,

Blown in on the strength of the breeze,
And because your Gods were duplicates
He shattered you on his knees.
I'll work my clay as I find it,
All hushed as it lies in the sod,
And he shall be built for better or worse
In the way of a Personal God.

Jungle Jargon

A monkey with a dreadful past
And sprawling bigotry of mind
Kept pinching all the cats behind
The scenery – it could not last.

It was a juggernaughty thing
Of jungles and of peasantry;
It laughed a little pleasantly,
It sang a song – it could not sing.

And down below where blind bears walk
Or lurch in tears upon a rug –
It is because they cannot hug,
It is because they cannot talk.

They are denied all things but weight
And rug value in days to come;
No wonder they are stricken dumb,
For this was never Dante's fate.

And, too, what lion has no wish
Napoleonlike to fold his hands
Upon its breast, to brew dread plans,
Or to receive a Judas kiss?

This Much and More

If my lover were a comet
　　Hung in air,
I would braid my leaping body
　　In his hair.

Yea, if they buried him ten leagues
　　Beneath the loam,
My fingers they would learn to dig
　　And I'd plunge home!

From Fifth Avenue Up

Someday beneath some hard
Capricious star –
Spreading its light a little
Over far,
We'll know you for the woman
That you are.

For though one took you, hurled you
Out of space,
With your legs half strangled
In your lace,
You'd lip the world to madness
On your face.

We'd see your body in the grass
With cool pale eyes.
We'd strain to touch those lang'rous
Length of thighs;
And hear your short sharp modern
Babylonic cries.

It wouldn't go. We'd feel you
Coil in fear
Leaning across the fertile
Fields to leer
As you urged some bitter secret
Through the ear.

We see your arms grow humid
In the heat;
We see your damp chemise lie
Pulsing in the beat
Of the over-hearts left oozing
At your feet.

See you sagging down with bulging
Hair to sip,
The dappled damp from some vague
Under lip.
Your soft saliva, loosed
With orgy, drip.

Once we'd not have called this
Woman you –
When leaning above your mother's
Spleen you drew
Your mouth across her breast as
Trick musicians do.

Plunging grandly out to fall
Upon your face.
Naked-female-baby
In grimace.
With your belly bulging stately
Into space.

In General

What altar cloth, what rag of worth
Unpriced?
What turn of card, with trick of game
Undiced?
And you we valued still a little
More than Christ.

From Third Avenue On

And now she walks on out turned feet
Beside the litter in the street
Or rolls beneath a dirty sheet
      Within the town.
She does not stir to doff her dress,
She does not kneel low to confess,
A little conscience, no distress
      And settles down.

Ah God! She settles down we say;
It means her powers slip away
It means she draws back day by day
      From good or bad.
And so she looks upon the floor
Or listens at an open door
Or lies her down, upturned to snore
      Both loud and sad.

Or sits beside the chinaware
Sits mouthing meekly in a chair,
With over-curled, hard waving hair
	Above her eyes.
Or grins too vacant into space –
A vacant space is in her face –
Where nothing came to take the place
	Of high hard cries.

Or yet we hear her on the stairs
With some few elements of prayers,
Until she breaks it off and swears
	A loved bad word.
Somewhere beneath her buried curse,
A corpse lies bounding in a hearse;
And friends and relatives disperse,
	And are not stirred.

Those living dead up in their rooms
Must note how partial are the tombs,
That take men back into the wombs
	While theirs must fast.
And those who have their blooms in jars
No longer stare into the stars,
Instead, they watch the dinky cars –
	And live aghast.

Seen from the 'L'

So she stands – nude – stretching dully
Two amber combs loll through her hair
A vague molested carpet pitches
Down the dusty length of stair.
She does not see, she does not care
      It's always there.

The frail mosaic on her window
Facing starkly towards the street
Is scribbled there by tipsy sparrows –
Etched there with their rocking feet.
Is fashioned too, by every beat
      Of shirt and sheet.

Still her clothing is less risky
Than her body in its prime,
They are chain-stitched and so is she
Chain-stitched to her soul for time.
Ravelling grandly into vice
Dropping crooked into rhyme.
Slipping through the stitch of virtue,
      Into crime.

Though her lips are vague and fancy
In her youth –
They bloom vivid and repulsive
As the truth.
Even vases in the making
      Are uncouth.

In Particular

What loin-cloth, what rag of wrong
Unpriced?
What turn of body, what of lust
Undiced?
So we've worshipped you a little
More than Christ.

Twilight of the Illicit

You, with your long blank udders
And your calms,
Your spotted linen and your
Slack'ning arms.
With satiated fingers dragging
At your palms.

Your knees set far apart like
Heavy spheres;
With discs upon your eyes like
Husks of tears;
And great ghastly loops of gold
Snared in your ears.

Your dying hair hand-beaten
'Round your head.
Lips, long lengthened by wise words
Unsaid.
And in your living all grimaces
Of the dead.

One sees you sitting in the sun
Asleep;
With the sweeter gifts you had
And didn't keep,
One grieves that the altars of
Your vice lie deep.

You, the twlight powder of
A fire-wet dawn;
You, the massive mother of
Illicit spawn;
While the others shrink in virtue
You have borne.

We'll see you staring in the sun
A few more years,
With discs upon your eyes like
Husks of tears;
And great ghastly loops of gold
Snared in your ears.

To a Cabaret Dancer

A thousand lights had smitten her
　　Into this thing;
Life had taken her and given her
　　One place to sing.

She came with laughter wide and calm;
　　And splendid grace;
And looked between the lights and wine
　　For one fine face.

And found life only passion wide
　　'Twixt mouth and wine.
She ceased to search, and growing wise
　　Became less fine.

Yet some wondrous thing within the mess
    Was held in check: –
Was missing as she groped and clung
    About his neck.

One master chord we couldn't sound
    For lost the keys,
Yet she hinted of it as she sang
    Between our knees.

We watched her come with subtle fire
    And learned feet,
Stumbling among the lustful drunk
    Yet somehow sweet

We saw the crimson leave her cheeks
    Flame in her eyes;
For when a woman lives in awful haste
    A woman dies.

The jests that lit out hours by night
    And made them gay,
Soiled a sweet and ignorant soul
    And fouled its play.

Barriers and heart both broken-dust
    Beneath her feet.
You've passed her forty times and sneered
    Out in the street.

A thousand jibes had driven her
    To this at last;
Till the ruined crimson of her lips
    Grew vague and vast.

Until her songless soul admits
    Time comes to kill:
You pay her price and wonder why
    You need her still.

Suicide

Corpse A
They brought her in, a shattered small
Cocoon,
With a little bruisèd body like
A startled moon;
And all the subtle symphonies of her
A twilight rune.

Corpse B
They gave her hurried shoves this way
And that.
Her body shock-abbreviated
As a city cat.
She lay out listlessly like some small mug
Of beer gone flat.

Death

Down the dusty highway, on the broken road,
   With curls as thin as smoke is hovering round his head,
Came the slow procession with its dreaming load:
   The man who stopped his living that he might be dead.

On the sodden plank-bridge, musing through the town,
   Thus, with hands before him, crossed like girls' who pray,
So the vivid corpse came, with his head bent down,
   In the chill of morning and through the common day.

Straight his lips, *sans* laughter, all the pain left in,
   Quiet as a chancel that breathes a morning prayer;
So the stately body, with its rigid chin
   And its startled, leaping-high, thin, damp curls of hair.

Thus does one consider, death and man debate,
   Some must leave to-morrow, but some must know to-day;
And some approach too early, but most approach too late,
   When the tang of random youth has dropped into decay.

Heavy feet, like women's hands pregnant with vast prayer,
   All his muted splendor caught upon Death's loom,
With his throat fast fettered to the branches of his hair,
   But with soul tobogganing upon the sled of doom.

Through the dark'ning city to a narrow space,
   With a song between his teeth, silence in control,
With a little humor clenched within his face
   And a little wonder wedged within his soul.

In Conclusion

Not every pipe is builded for our lays,
  Some hour the echo of our feet will flee,
  For, all unenvied, high eternity
Is deep with those who leave eternal ways.

No hate, no love, and no parental prayer
  Lives in the young; old wines they do not hold,
  And hate and love are outlived by the old –
Too near to death for passion and despair.

And we who live our time alway too fast,
  Whose lips beneath the kiss fall into dust,
  Will feel on the blade of Time untimely rust,
So all of us outlive our hearts at last.

Yet I who loved, and you who loved, and all
  Who rose most steeply and were not above
  Great human pity and inhuman love,
Will not be found ignoble when we fall.

Dust

The Nation falls. And still the Hosts arise
    To walk above this hemisphere of pain,
Built by the voice of man. Indebted to those eyes
That bled the mind's deep blood of old surprise
That nothing lives, and nothing ever dies.

*   *   *   *   *   *

As once, this road we walk each hour above
    Was every hour prostrate before the Lord,
The leveled prayer of some too human flame –
    An Idol dropped to dust while still adored.

And so it is for every temple praised
    Some whispered penance to the dust is flung
And there to cleave, until some wo shall stir
    The cloistered ashes of that anguished tongue.

And I, who in mine own grave am a guest,
    Am stranger in myself as absolute.
    I banquet at myself in high dispute
And to myself pledge wines still unaddressed.

So all who have been flung up from the Pangs,
    And, by some Hand retossed before the fruit
Will once again be found beneath that flower
    Within the clenched fingers of its root.

And I – I, too, am falling to that height
    One with the Kneeling, emptied of their breath
For you who walk above, to call it Dust –
    For us below, the Miracle of Death.

Birth

Fore-loved, fore-crowned, and fore-betrayed,
   And thrice our quality been weighed,
  And thrice our hearts been spit with steel
  To prove us worthier to feel
Both love and hate creep through that blade,
   The wings of doom press tip to tip,
And all dead hands like bricks are laid
  And reach like mansions to the sky –
   The parting, weeping lip to lip,
That all things born must alway die.
And that the seed of Nothing lies
  Yet here within this envied Much –
  So we are forecast, and of such
The child's first sobbing prophesies.

The Yellow Jar

White butterflies are creeping near
  This yellow jar where rose-leaves lie,
Like simple nuns in gowns of fear,
  Like humor and like tragedy.

And down they steal with throbbing wing
  Across the pool of shadows, where
That other bowl of dust is king
  With blossoms past, with tear, with prayer.

One was the rose you brought, and one
  Was you. The symbol lied – it seemed
You were the summit of the sun;
  Now you are less than that you dreamed.

In life we loved you, and in death
  There is devotion for you, too;
Only the witless human breath
  Is mourning for the death in you.

Yet what of you, I wonder, stands
  Without the stillness of the room,
Beyond the reach of rising hands,
  Still smiling at this china tomb!

White butterflies are creeping past
  The jar of death, the yellow jar;
For butterflies are not the last
  To sense things are not as they are!

The Last Toast

My tears are falling one by one
Upon the silence of this bed;
Like rain they crown his quiet head,
Like moons they slip within his hair;
They came like wine and passed like prayer
Into the goblets of the dead.

To an Idol

It sat with folded hands and grinned
  Upon our sky.
Each ocher lock that streaked its head
  Was curled and dry.
A little dust of aged despair
  Was in each eye.

Both somber wooden breasts seemed weighed
  With heavy tears,
Dropped and forgotten long ago
  In other years,
But waiting still to fall like fate
  Upon the ears.

Beneath its girdle and its chains
  Each carved foot stood;
Incapable of pangs or pains,
  Or sweats of blood.
Conceived in superstition
  And doomed in wood.

And yet behind abysmal leer
  And faulty frown,
Throbbing faintly out of space
  That shadows drown –
We hear God's grim machinery
  Run down.

Shadows

A little trellis stood beside my head,
And all the tiny fruitage of its vine
Fashioned a shadowy cover to my bed,
And I was madly drunk on shadow wine!

A lily bell hung sidewise, leaning down,
And gowned me in a robe so light and long;
And so I dreamed, and drank, and slept, and heard
The lily's song.

Lo, for a house, the shadow of the moon;
For golden money, all the daisy rings;
And for my love, the meadow at my side –
Thus tramps are kings!

Love Song

I am the woman – it is I –
Through all my pain I suffer peace;
Through all my peace I suffer pain;
This insufficient agony –
This stress of wo I cannot feel –
These knees that cannot bend to kneel –
A corpse that flames and cannot die –
A candle with the wick torn through –
These are the things from which I grew
Into the woman whom you hate –
She whom you loved before you knew –
Loved, loved so much before you knew.

All I cannot weep – in tears,
All I cannot pray – in prayers;
For it is so the wild world moves,
And it is so that Tame Man loves.
It is for this books fall to ruin;
For this great houses mold and fall;
For this the infant gown, the pall;
For this the veil that eyes weep through;
For this the birds go stumbling down
Into the cycled ages where
Their squandered plumage rends the air.
For this each living thing that dies
Shakes loose a soul that will arise
Like ivory against black space –
A quiet thing, but with a face
Wherein a weeping mouth is built –
A little wound where grief is spilt.

I am the woman – even so –
Through the years I have not swerved,
Through the years I've altered not.
What changes have I yet to know?
Through what gardens must I crawl?
How many roses yet must fall?
How many flowers yet must blow?
How many blossoms yet must rot?
How many thorns must I yet bear
Within the clenched fists of despair?
To be again she whom you loved –
Loved you so much, so much did care –
Loved, loved so much, so much did care!

Lines to a Lady

Lay her under the rusty grass,
   With her two eyes heavy and blind and done;
Her two hands crossed beneath her breast
   One on one.

Lay her out in the paling eve,
   With its sudden tears and white birch-trees;
And let her passing seem to be
   One with these.

Close her out of this hour of grief,
   And casting the earth on her, like a breath,
Sew her tenderly, that she may
   Reap her death!

And close her eyes, close, close her lips,
   For still, too still is her smitten tongue;
Her hour's over, her breath has passed,
   And her song is sung.

Lay her under the wild red grass
   In the fields death-tossed and bowed with rain;
And let her silence seem to move
   Within the grain.

The Lament of Women

Ah My God!

Ah my God, what is it that we love!
This flesh laid on us like a wrinkled glove?
Bones caught in haste from out some lustful bed,
And for momentum, this a devil's shove.

What is it that hurriedly we kiss,
This mouth that seeks our own, or still more this
Small sorry eye within the cheated head,
As if it mourned the something that we miss.

This pale, this over eager listening ear
The wretched mouth its soft lament to hear,
To mark the noiseless and the anguished fall
Of still one other warm misshapen tear.

Short arms, and bruised feet long set apart
To walk with us forever from the start.
Ah God, is this the reason that we love –
Because such things are death blows to the heart?

To the Hands of a Beloved

His hands, I love to think, have left some trace
On some white wall or dusty balustrade.
Good, eager hands, cast outward for a space
And touching things a little ere they fade
And fall and are with death anointed and dismayed.

I like to think that some day as I pass
This tall and somber mirror I shall win
The touch of his quick fingers from the glass
When, searching in his face for what had been,
He paused here utterly confounded, looking in.

On some object, unnoticed, cast aside,
Some hour he'll strike with careless palm outspread,
And there'll remain of him, though he had died,
A memory that shall lift him from the dead;
And weeping between my hands, I shall be comforted.

To One in Favour

When the throne stands empty, and the king goes down,
  Down into the darkness by your high white tent,
And shall sheath his gray sword, lay aside his crown;
  Then, O tall white woman, shall you be content?

Shall you be contented, lying on his knee,
  Murmuring face downward, lips within his palm?
Then shall you remember, thus you once kissed me,
  Only wilder, madder, closer in my arm?

When he shall release you, turn his eyes to sleep;
  Will you lift a little, looking in his face,
And recall out parting, for a moment weep
  Down upon his doublet, tarnishing the lace?

And when up the sun rides, and the daylight comes,
  Loud with sudden sparrows, and their latest talk,
Will you take his face so, in your two long thumbs
  Kiss his mouth for kindness, then rise up and walk?

To a Bird

Up from some leafy cover hot with June
　And odorous with spicy mysteries
　Of herbs unknown, a red bird dipping flies,
Whistling a little sadly, out of tune,
　　　Under a slow moon.

Lifts and turns, and, like blots on a wall,
　Leaves fleeting shadows in its drowsy flight;
　The earth beneath, and all above the night,
And stealing out between the last leaf's fall
　　　A new bird's call.

Singing its way into the South once more,
　No more returning; and the dropping leaves
　The branches strip like arms thrust out of sleeves –
And though the wind doth through the whole world roar
　　　A feather only stirs upon its floor.

To the Dead Favourite of Liu Ch'e

The sound of rustling silk is stilled,
With solemn dust the court is filled,
No footfalls echo on the floor;
A thousand leaves stop up her door,
Her little golden drink is spilled.

Her painted fan no more shall rise
Before her black barbaric eyes –
The scattered tea goes with the leaves.
And simply crossed her yellow sleeves;
And every day a sunset dies.

Her birds no longer coo and call,
The cherry blossoms fade and fall,
Nor ever does her shadow stir
But stares forever back at her,
And through her runs no sound at all.

And bending low, my falling tears
Drop fast against her little ears,
And yet no sound comes back, and I
Who used to play her tenderly
Have touched her not a thousand years.

To One Feeling Differently

To-night I cannot know you and I weep
For sorrow that's upon you like soft sleep
Of which alone you are the one possessed –
And as one in long stuff of mourning dressed –
Drenched deep in garments that take shape of grief
Fold on heavy fold, as leaf on leaf.
You stand, all tremulous with stifled cries,
And with chill tears like glass upon your eyes.
Thin shadows, darker than the darkness boil
With foamy somnolence and monstrous toil
The solemn lisping of untimely things
Approaches; and on high lamenting wings
Cold time screams past us, shedding sparks of pain –
Of which you are the core and the refrain.

She Passed This Way

Here where the trees still tremble with your flight
I sit and braid thin whips to beat you down.
How shall we ever find you who have gone
In little dresses, lisping through the town?

Great men on horses hunt you, and strong boys
Employ their arrows in the shallow air.
But I shall be heard whistling where I follow
Braiding long wisps of grass and stallion's hair.

And in the night when thirty hawks are high
In pendent rhythm, and all the wayside loud;
When they are burning field and bush and hedge,
I'll steal you like a penny from the crowd.

Crystals

Wax-heavy, snared in age-splintered linen, the king's daughter;
The shimmer of her eyeballs blue beneath the lids like
             thin rain water.
Small and sour the lemon blossoms banked at the breast-bone;
Her two breasts dark of death, and stained a dark tone.
Her lips flower-tarnished, her cheek-braids bulked in rust.
Her shoulders as hard as a wall-tree, frosted with dust.
Precise bone clipped and grooved, and as sure as metal.
Leaves of flesh built high, like china roses, petal on petal.
Odor of apples rising from the death robes chinks and breaks.
Seeds of pepper falling down from brittle, spiced womb- cakes.
Her swift cunning impaled on her brain's darkness. She died
Of her heart's sharp crystal spiral pricked in her side.
Six tomb-Gods in basalt make her one of these –
Who lie a million years, listening for thieves.

The Child Would Be Older

Cold tears, my brave man? Come, my
  little garçon,
I'll take you to my girl's breast, and sing
  you a war-song.
Where the horses gather, listen to their
  hoofs strike.
What is a pigeon or a scythe within the
  wheat like?
Oh, the single, cool thought that we string
  in childhood,
As clean and as brittle as a small stick of
  hard-wood.
Now it is a massacre, a scandal, or a pen-
  chant.
I'll cut you down a clear curl, to thicken
  out your swan-song.

To One in Another Mood

O Dear beloved, shall I not go back
From gazing on you always with wet eyes,
And mournful kisses from these lips where lies
More honey than your aloes? Must I crack
Still darker herbs, and sighing keep the track
With feigned lamenting and with fearful cries,
Slow twining you about with blasphemies
Because I would be dancing? Nay, I lack
The needed dull intoning of despair.
Nor in me echoes your too sombre mood,
Nor is it in my heart. Nor anywhere
Within my flesh the very flesh you wooed.
Then wherefore shall I loose my braided hair
Hiding my eyes, pretending that I brood?

I'd Have You Think of Me

As one who, leaning on the wall, once drew
Thick blossoms down, and harkened to
      the hum
Of heavy bees slow rounding the wet plum,
And heard across the fields the patient coo
Of restless birds bewildered with the dew.

As one whose thoughts were mad in painful May,
With melancholy eyes turned toward her love,
And toward the troubled earth whereunder
  throve
The chilly rye and coming hawthorn spray –
With one lean, pacing hound, for company.

The Flowering Corpse

So still she lies in this closed place apart,
Her feet grown fragile for the ghostly tryst;
Her pulse no longer striking in her wrist,
Nor does its echo wander through her heart.

Over the body and the quiet head
Like stately ferns above an austere tomb,
Soft hairs blow; and beneath her armpits bloom
The drowsy passion flowers of the dead.

Song in Autumn

The wind comes down before the creeping night
And you, my love, are hid within the green
Long grasses; and the dark steals up between
Each leaf, as through the shadow quick with fright
The startled hare leaps up and out of sight.

The hedges whisper in their loaded boughs
Where warm birds slumber, pressing wing to wing,
All pulsing faintly, like a muted string
Above us where we weary of our vows –
And hidden underground the soft moles drowse.

First Communion

The mortal fruit upon the bough
Hangs above the nuptial bed.
The cat-bird in the tree returns
The forfeit of his mutual vow.

The hard, untimely apple of
The branch that feeds on watered rain
Takes the place upon her lips
Of her late lamented love.

Many hands together press
Shaped within a static prayer
Recall to one the chorister
Docile in his sexless dress.

The temperate winds reclaim the iced
Remorseless vapours of the snow.
The only pattern in the mind
Is the cross behind the Christ.

Hush Before Love

A voice rose in the darkness saying
    'Love,'
And in the stall the scattered mice grew
    still,
Where yet the white ox slept, and on the sill
The crowing cock paused, and the grey house
  dove
Turned twice about upon the ledge above.

Antique

A lady in a cawl of lawn
With straight bound tabs and muted eyes,
And lips fair thin and deftly drawn
    And oddly wise.

A cameo, a ruff of lace,
A neck cut square with corners laid;
A thin Greek nose and near the face
    A polished braid.

Low, sideways looped, of amber stain
The pale ears caught within its snare.
A profile like a dagger lain
    Between the hair.

Pastoral

A frog leaps out across the lawn,
And crouches there – all heavy and alone,
And like a blossom, pale and over-blown,
Once more the moon turns dim against the dawn.

Crawling across the straggling panoply
Of little roses, only half in bloom,
It strides within that beamed and lofty room
Where an ebon stallion looms upon the hay.

The stillness moves, and seems to grow immense,
A shudd'ring dog starts, dragging at its chain,
Thin, dusty rats slink down within the grain,
And in the vale the first far bells commence.

Here in the dawn, with mournful doomed eyes
A cow uprises, moving out to bear
A soft-lipped calf with swarthy birth-swirled hair,
And wide wet mouth, and droll uncertainties.

The grey fowls fight for places in the sun,
The mushrooms flare, and pass like painted fans:
All the world is patient in its plans –
The seasons move forever, one on one.

Small birds lie sprawling vaguely in the heat,
And wanly pluck at shadows on their breasts,
And where the heavy grape-vine leans and rests,
White butterflies lift up their furry feet.

The wheat grows querulous with unseen cats;
A fox strides out in anger through the corn,
Bidding each acre wake and rise to mourn
Beneath its sharps and through its throaty flats.

And so it is, and will be year on year,
Time in and out of date, and still on time
A billion grapes plunge bleeding into wine
And bursting, fall like music on the ear.

The snail that marks the girth of night with slime,
The lonely adder hissing in the fern,
The lizard with its ochre eyes aburn –
Each is before, and each behind its time.

Paradise

This night I've been one hour in Paradise;
There found a feather from the Cock
    that Crew –
There heard the echo of the Kiss that Slew,
And in the dark, about past agonies
    Hummed little flies.

Six Songs of Khalidine

To the Memory of Mary Pyne

The flame of your red hair does crawl and creep
Upon your body that denies the gloom
And feeds upon your flesh as 't would consume
The cold precision of your austere sleep –
And all night long I beat it back, and weep.

It is not gentleness but mad despair
That sets us kissing mouths, O Khalidine,
Your mouth and mine, and one sweet mouth
      unseen
We call our soul. Yet thick within our hair
The dusty ashes that our days prepare.

The dark comes up, my little love, and dyes
Your fallen lids with stain of ebony,
And draws a thread of fear 'tween you and me
Pulling thin blindness down across our eyes –
And far within the vale a lost bird cries.

Does not the wind moan round your painted
      towers
Like rats within an empty granary?
The clapper lost, and long blown out to sea
Your windy doves. And here the black bat
      cowers
Against your clock that never strikes the hours.

And now I say, has not the mountain's base
Here trembled long ago unto the cry
'I love you, ah, I love you!' Now we die
And lay, all silent, to the earth our face.
Shall that cast out the echo of this place?

Has not one in the dark funereal
Heard foot-fall fearful, born of no man's tread,
And felt the wings of death, though no wing
    spread
And on his cheek a tear, though no tear fell –
And a voice saying without breath 'Farewell!'

Lullaby

When I was young child I slept with a dog,
I lived without trouble and I thought no harm;
I ran with the boys and I played leap-frog;
Now it is a girl's head that lies on my arm.

Then I grew a little, picked plantain in the yard;
Now I dwell in Greenwich, and the people do not call;
Then I planted pepper-seed and stamped on them hard.
Now I am very quiet and I hardly plan at all.

Then I pricked my finger on a thorn, or a thistle,
Put the finger in my mouth, and ran to my mother.
Now I lie here, with my eyes on a pistol.
There will be a morrow, and another, and another.

Finis

For you, for me? Why then the striking
      hour,
The wind among the curtains, and the
      tread
Of some late gardener pulling at the flower
They'll lay between our hearts when we are dead.

Quarry

While I unwind duration from the tongue-tied tree,
Send carbon fourteen down for time's address.
The old revengeful without memory
Stand by –
I come, I come that path and there look in
And see the capsized eye of sleep and wrath
And hear the beaters' 'Gone to earth!'
Then do I sowl the soul and slap its face
That it fetch breath.

The Walking-Mort

Call her walking-mort; say where she goes
She squalls her bush with blood. I slam a gate
Report her axis bone it gigs the rose.
What say of mine? It turns a grinning grate.
Impugn her that she baits time with an awl.
What do my sessions then? They task a grave.
So, shall we stand, or shall we tread and wait
The mantled lumber of the buzzard's fall
(That maiden resurrection and the freight),
Or shall we freeze and wrangle by the wall?

Rite of Spring

Man cannot purge his body of its theme
As can the silkworm on a running thread
Spin a shroud to re-consider in.

Creatures in an Alphabet

The adder in the grass can hiss
The lynxes in the dark can kiss
Each otter holds his otter's hand
For this is how the Lord has planned.

Alas!

When hovering, the Hummingbird
Is always going home (it's said).
By flying in a single spot
It's striving fast to think it's not.

With cloven lip, with baleful eye,
The Camel wears the caliph high.
But though he do the master's will,
He himself's his habit still.

Why is it the Donkey haws,
And backs away (the mule) because
Although it hasn't said it's who,
It's practising *solfeggio*.

The reason that the Elephant
Is both detained and yet at ease,
Is because it is four trees
That the Lord forgot to plant.

The Fish, the Fish, how is he caught?
With grave intent, or so we thought;
Yet with what a flattened look
It goes fishing, without hook.

The trim Giraffe, on ankles slight,
Dips its crown in pale moonlight;
But what it poles for, none can say –
It's much too up and high away.

The Hippo is a wading junk,
A sort of Saratoga trunk
With all its trappings on its back,
Through which the birds of passage peck.

When from mischief interdict,
The Imago perfected rise,
And lays it's dool at Heaven's Gate,
Then in this alphabet it is.

Though it be loud with auguries
Of summer sun, and happy days;
Nonetheless the Blue Jay is
Lined with insect agonies.

The Kinkajou, the hanging sloth,
Or any else that looks uncouth,
Aren't they somewhat upside down?
Or are they merely three of both?

Horrid hunger is the cause,
That opens up the Lion's jaws;
Yet what it tears apart for meat
Is merely what its victims ate.

In the zoo the Monkeys screech
At any dainty out of reach;
Yet let a corpulence be found,
They whack it madly to the ground.

If ascension is your hope,
Ride not the Nigor (antelope)
But mount the springbok for the run;
It jumps straight up, like hot popcorn.

When musing on the Ocelot,
Or on the panther's hurling tail,
One wonders how such stealth is caught,
And how it be the cats prevail.

If among itself it go,
(As the Peacock's said to do),
With all its thousand eyes ajar,
Is it itself it's looking for?

Now for quidnunc, now for Quail,
(One runs off, the others rail);
But what about? It ends the same –
An old man's titter, a young man's game.

What of Raccoon, animal?
With visor down (or domino),
When at *ombre* or *quadrille*,
Will it vail and let you know?

The Seal, she lounges like a bride,
Much too docile, there's no doubt;
Madame Récamier, on side,
(If such she has), and bottom out.

'Tyger! Tyger!' – Who wrote that?
You won't take it with your hat,
Nor lure it with a golden cage;
It won't leap its master's page.

Unicorn, the one-horned beast
Mistranslated from the start,
(See Deuteronomy, at least),
An upright, but a much vex'd art.

Now of the Vesper Wasp beware,
Its butt and bust hang by an hair,
Its sting's a death; otherwise
It's riggish in its enterprise.

Somewhat sullen, many days,
The Walrus is a cow that neighs.
Tusked, ungainly, and windblown,
It sits on ice, and alone.

As there was nothing more to say,
The X has crossed himself away.
And as there's nothing new to prove,
He marked his exit with his love.

A bale of hair, the Yak he be,
His bitter butter minged in tea;
With all his craggy services,
His lowly life Himalayan is.

('Round the mulberry we go.)

When the Kissing Flesh is Gone

When the kissing flesh is gone
And tooth to tooth true lovers lie
Idly snarling, bone to bone,
Will you term that ecstasy?

Nay, but love in chancery.
In the last extremity,
Duelling eternity,
Love lies down in clemency,
Compounding rogue fidelity.

Portrait of a Lady Walking

In the North birds feather a long wind.
She is beautiful.
The Fall lays ice on the lemon's rind.
Her slow ways are attendant on the dark mind.
The frost sets a brittle stillness on the pool.
Onto the cool short pile of the wet grass
Birds drop like a shower of glass.

Lament for Wretches, Every One

As whales by dolphins slashed, bring on a school
Of lesser fins to passenger the blood,
So comes my general man, both my priest, and hood
To ask, 'who drank baptism down in nothing flat?
Who cut the comb in half to see it quick
With buzzing backsides, quartered out of cells?
And sick
And staggered regents staling pedestals?'
I replied:
'What heard of Darkness oysters in your tide?'

As Cried

And others ask, 'What's it to be possessed
Of one you cannot keep, she being old?'
There is no robin in my eye to build a nest
For any bride who shakes against the cold,
Nor is there a claw that would arrest
– I keep the hoof from stepping on her breath –
The ravelled clue that dangles crock by a thread,
Who hooked her to the underworld. I said in a breath
I keep a woman, as all do, feeding death.

As Cried

'If gold falls sick, being stung by mercury'
What then, being stung by treason and surprise?
Will turn its other cheek?
And He replies (who is misquoted ere he speak),
'Why She
Who keeps the minerals of Paradise.'

Discant (There should be gardens)

There should be gardens for old men
To twitter in;
Boscage too, for *Madames*, sports
For memory, poor puff-balls of a day;
Soundless virginals laid on to ply
Suet to eat, and herbs to make them spin
Cuttle and costard on a plate, loud hay
To start the gnat – and then
Mulberry, to re-consider in –
Resign? Repent?
Observe the *haute* meander of pavan
But never ask the one-foot snail
Which way you went.

Satires (Satires of Don Pasquin)

Man cannot purge his body of its theme,
As does the silk-worm ferry forth her thread,
High Commander, tell me what is man
And what surmise?
Is breastmilk in the lamentation yet?
O predacious victim of the wheel,
St. Catherine of roses, turn your gaze
Where woe is;
Purge the body of its dread,
As does the bombace from her furnance heave
To weave a shroud to metamorphose in?
To re-consider in
What bolt of havoc holds your dread?
On what cast of terror are you fed?

Discontent

Truly, when I pause and stop to think
That with an hempen rope I'll spool to bed,
Aware that tears of mourners on the brink
Are merely spindrift of the shaken head,
Then, as the squirrel quarreling his nut,
I with my winter store am in dispute,
For none will burrow in to share my bread.

Dereliction

Does the inch-worm on the Atlas mourn
That last acre its not inched upon?
As does the rascal, when to grass he's toed
Thunder in the basket, mowed to measure;
The four last things begun:
Leviathan
Thrashing on the banks of kingdomcome.

Dereliction (Augusta said)

Augusta *said*:
'Had I foresight of the mole
I'd have taken my paps underground
Papp'd and staked like a coachmans coat.
There suckled darkness, and the goat;
As women must,
Who suckle dust.'

Dereliction and Virgin Spring

ITEM:

Tell where is the kissing-crust
Where three labours met; the trine
Father, Son and Ghost?
Not a crumb.
Who broke the bonding of that loaf apart?
Who drank the wine?
Who took the peel
And turn'd the Host on his own heel?
Who made the sign?
Who is the moocher with the down turn'd thumb?
Who capsized Jehovah in a ditch
At Gath?
Leviathan
Thrashing on the wharf at kingdomcome?

Laughing Lamentations of Dan Corbeau

Observe where Corbeau hops, touches his fly
With cold, fastidious alarm, and piping forth
Flora, with the sweet sap-sucking cry
'What, kiss the famine of an old man's mouth!'
That party's 'game' as mystery is posed in truth
'High' as a partridge on a peg is 'high.'
'Rather will I eat my fists in youth!'
So let them go, for God's sake; I'd as lief
She get my wisdom on a shorter tooth,
Nor shall I 'eat my other hand for grief.'

The Bo Tree

All children, at some time, and hand in hand
Go to the woods to be un-parented
And ministered in the leaves. The frozen bole
The spirit kicks in spring, will that amend
The winter in the hearse? Pick from his hole
The daub was Caesar? Will the damned
Who rake the sparrows bones the fires burn black,
Find the pilgrim down, a tree stuck in their backs?

Discant (His mother said)

His mother said
(Who long since in her mother is been hid)
'I am the birth-place of the dead.'
'Indeed' he said
'Let it be done;
Let us give our tigers, each one to the other one.'

Discant (He said to the Don)

He said to the Don, 'My Lord
Your dangling man's not crucified
He's gored.'
The picador replied:
'Truth is an handled fruit:
Isn't that your finger in His side?'

Verse

Should any ask 'what is it to be in love
With one you cannot slough, she being young?'
What should it be, we answer, who can prove
The falling of the milk-tooth on the tongue,
Is autumn in the mouth enough.

Therefore Sisters

Therefore sisters now begin
With time-locked heel
To mourn the vanishing and mewing;
Taboo becomes obscene from too much wooing:
Glory rots, like any other green.

Therefore daughters of the Gwash
Look not for Orpheus the swan
Nor wash
The Traveller his boot
Both are gone.

Laughing Lamentations

Lord, what is man, that he was once your brag?
A spawling job of flesh with off-set thumb.
Grown so insolent he lifts his leg
Upon the running sessions of his tomb.
And where's the black purse was his mother's bag?
(It coined his faces, both sides, good and ill,)
Why round his neck it bangs for begging bread,
Her Merry thought? The skipjack of the kill.

Fyfield*Books*

Two millennia of essential classics

The extensive Fyfield*Books* list includes

For more information, including a full list of Fyfield*Books* and a contents list for each title, and details of how to order the books in the UK, visit the Fyfield website at www.fyfieldbooks.co.uk or email info@fyfieldbooks.co.uk. For information about Fyfield*Books* available in the United States and Canada, visit the Routledge website at www.routledge-ny.com.